MONARCH BUTTERFLY MIGRATION

BY REBECCA HIRSCH

The Child's World®

Published by The Child's World®
1980 Lookout Drive • Mankato, MN 56003-1705
800-599-READ • www.childsworld.com

ACKNOWLEDGMENTS
The Child's World®: Mary Berendes, Publishing Director
Content Consultant: Dr. Tanya Dewey,
    University of Michigan Museum of Zoology
The Design Lab: Design and production
Red Line Editorial: Editorial direction

PHOTO CREDITS
Oleg Kulakov/Dreamstime, cover (top), 1, back cover; Jodi Jacobson/
iStockphoto, cover (bottom), 2–3; Tony Campbell/Shutterstock Images, 4–5;
The Design Lab, 7; Jill Lang/iStockphoto, 8–9; Cathy Keifer/Shutterstock
Images, 10 (bottom), 20–21; Steve Greer/iStockphoto, 10–11 (top); Joyce
Boffert/Shutterstock Images, 12–13; Jacob Hamblin/Shutterstock Images, 14;
Megan R. Hoover/Shutterstock Images, 15; Ken Kistler/Shutterstock Images,
16; David Vadala/Shutterstock Images, 17; Simon Phipps/iStockphoto,
18–19; Cathy Keifer/iStockphoto, 22; Jill Kyle/iStockphoto, 24; Shutterstock
Images, 27; Jody Van Slembrouck/Fotolia, 28

Design elements: Oleg Kulakov/Dreamstime

ISBN 9781609736248
LCCN 2011940087

Printed in the United States of America

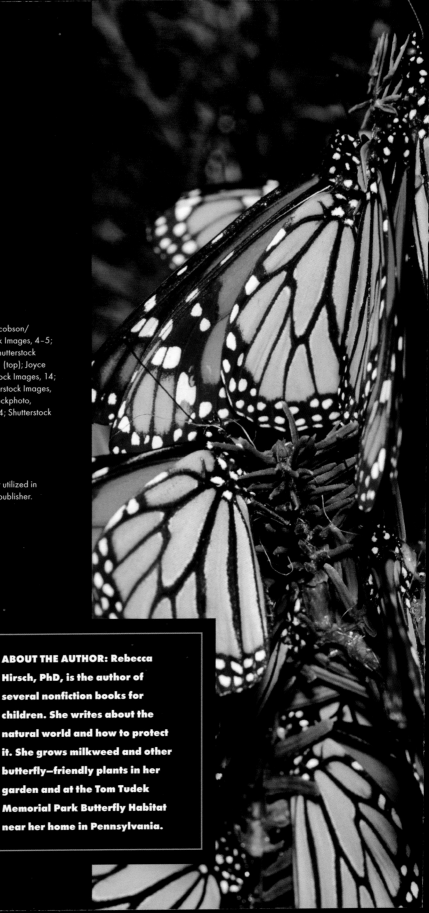

ABOUT THE AUTHOR: Rebecca Hirsch, PhD, is the author of several nonfiction books for children. She writes about the natural world and how to protect it. She grows milkweed and other butterfly—friendly plants in her garden and at the Tom Tudek Memorial Park Butterfly Habitat near her home in Pennsylvania.

TABLE OF CONTENTS

MONARCH BUTTERFLIES...4

MIGRATION MAP...6

BECOMING A BUTTERFLY...8

LIFE IN THE SUMMER...12

FLYING SOUTH...14

FINDING THEIR WAY...17

MONARCH WINTERS...18

FLYING BACK NORTH...22

HABITAT THREATS...25

TYPES OF MIGRATION...30

GLOSSARY...31

FURTHER INFORMATION...32

INDEX...32

MONARCH BUTTERFLIES

Every fall something wonderful happens across North America. Millions of monarch butterflies from across North America fly south. They travel up to 3,000 miles (4,800 km). They fly all the way to Mexico, Florida, and Southern California. The monarch's black and orange wings look delicate. They are very strong, though. Monarch butterflies complete the longest journey of any insect on Earth.

The monarchs' lifetime journey is their migration. This is when an animal moves from one **habitat** to another. Migrations happen for many reasons. Some animals move to be in warmer weather where there is more food. There they can reproduce, or have their babies. And these migrations can be short distances, such as from a mountaintop to its valley. Or they can be long distances, like the monarch's flight.

A monarch butterfly has strong wings.

MIGRATION MAP

Monarch butterflies fly by several paths on their **seasonal** migration. Monarchs by the Great Lakes fly straight toward Texas and Mexico. Monarchs in New England fly along the coast of the Atlantic Ocean. Monarchs in the West follow the coast of the Pacific Ocean.

The monarchs from the middle and eastern parts of North America end up in central Mexico and Florida. The monarchs from western North America travel to southern California. Some go to western parts of Mexico for the winter.

This map shows the migration routes of monarch butterflies.

CANADA

U. S. A.

MEXICO

A female monarch butterfly lays her eggs on a milkweed plant.

EACH FEMALE MONARCH
ONLY LAYS ONLY ONE EGG
ON A MILKWEED PLANT.

BECOMING A BUTTERFLY

Monarchs live in fields, meadows, and gardens. Life begins on a milkweed plant. It is the monarch butterfly's **host plant**. A female butterfly finds a milkweed plant. She is ready to lay her eggs. She chooses a leaf near the top of the plant. She glues one egg to the underside of the leaf.

After a few days the egg **hatches**. A caterpillar crawls out. The caterpillar eats and grows. First it eats its eggshell. Then it eats the milkweed plant. The caterpillar needs to grow and store energy. It needs energy for its **metamorphosis**. This is its change from a caterpillar to a butterfly. The caterpillar **molts** as it grows. It spins some silk. It sticks the silk to a leaf. Then it wiggles out of its old skin. Fresh new skin is underneath.

A monarch caterpillar eats the milkweed plant's leaves.

Monarch caterpillars change into butterflies.

Monarch caterpillars have colors on their bodies. The colors warn **predators**. The caterpillars eat only milkweed. They absorb milkweed poisons into their bodies. The poisons do not harm the caterpillars. The poisons can make birds and other animals sick, though. Predators stay away from the brightly striped caterpillars.

The caterpillar is ready for a big change in its body. It hangs upside down and sheds its skin one last time. It is now a **pupa**. The pupa's skin becomes a pale green **chrysalis**. Two weeks pass. The pupa's body changes inside the chrysalis. Then the chrysalis splits open. An adult butterfly crawls out. It hangs upside down to dry its wings. Then it flies off to look for food.

FEMALE BUTTERFLIES
CAN TASTE A PLANT
BY STANDING ON
IT. THEY TASTE WITH
ALL SIX LEGS.

*Adult butterflies get
their food from flowers.*

12

LIFE IN THE SUMMER

An adult butterfly is not a picky eater. It drinks **nectar** from many kinds of flowers. It spots the flowers with its eyes. It finds the nectar on the flower using its feet. Its feet and **antennae** have parts that sense taste. The butterfly uncurls its long **proboscis**. It sucks the sweet nectar from the flower. It **basks** in the sunshine and flaps its wings. This is how it warms its body.

Adult butterflies need to mate to make new butterflies. A male and a female come together to mate. Soon eggs grow in the female's body. Then she searches for milkweed plants to lay her eggs.

Monarch butterflies spend their summers in the meadows. But in late summer, life in the meadow changes. The days get shorter. Cool breezes blow. Winter is on its way. Monarchs cannot survive the freezing northern winters. They must leave their summer habitat. They fly south to survive the winter.

New butterflies in the
fall look the same, but
they do not mate or
lay eggs right away.

14

FLYING SOUTH

New butterflies grow in late summer. They look the same as other monarchs, but they are different. They do not mate or lay eggs right away. But they do eat a lot of nectar. They store the food as fat in their bodies.

Then these butterflies fly in one direction. They head for Mexico, Florida, or southern California. The butterflies travel about 40 to 100 miles (64 to 160 km) a day. More butterflies join the migration each week. Great clouds of butterflies can be seen in the sky.

Monarchs do not fly in flocks like birds. Each butterfly flies alone. Migrating monarchs soar very high in the sky. They ride air currents. These currents give them a push as they head south.

Even though they migrate at the same time, each monarch flies alone.

The monarchs gather in trees at night. They sit in big groups on the branches. This is called roosting. Thousands of monarch butterflies may roost in one tree. They bask in the morning sunlight. Their muscles warm up for another day of flight.

The monarchs stop for food along their journey.

FINDING THEIR WAY

No one knows how monarchs find their way. Scientists think monarchs use the sun to point the way. The sun moves across the sky. It rises in the east and sets in the west. The butterflies do not follow the sun from east to west, but they may use the sun to find their way. They can tell the time by using their antennae. The antennae can sense where the sun is in the sky. To fly south, the butterflies keep the sun on their left in the morning. In the late afternoon, they keep the sun on their right. Monarchs may also sense the magnetic field inside Earth. This field is what makes a compass point north. The butterflies may have a sort of compass in their bodies.

Butterflies live in different places. But many fly to the same place. They fly in different directions. A monarch in North Dakota flies straight to the south. But one in Indiana flies in a curve to get south. Somehow they all fly in the right direction. These monarch butterflies have never been to their winter homes before.

The sun may be used by monarchs to help guide them south.

MONARCH WINTERS

In Mexico, all the monarchs go to a few steep mountain ranges. They find the mountain forests. These forests are filled with a type of fir tree. It is called oyamel. The monarchs gather in the trees. There are thousands of monarchs. The butterflies hang from the trunks, branches, and needles. The oyamel branches bend with the weight of the butterflies. Sometimes the branches even break. It sends the butterflies crashing to the ground.

The western monarchs spend their winters in Southern California. The coastal forests there have weather like the Mexican forests.

The mountain forests seem like a strange place for monarchs to spend the winter. There is less food for them to eat. The air in the forest is chilly. It is between 32 and 60 °F (0 and 15 °C). Sometimes it even drops below freezing. Why would butterflies travel to a place that is cold? Why would they travel to a place without enough food?

In their winter homes, monarchs gather on trees.

UP TO 15,000 MONARCHS CAN
CLUSTER ON ONE FIR BRANCH.

But the mountain forests are perfect for the monarchs. The forests keep the monarchs safe. The oyamel trees grow close together. Their branches touch. This keeps out deadly winter storms. Fog and clouds settle over the forest. They bring moist air. It keeps the butterflies from drying out.

It is too cold for the butterflies to fly. So, they hang in the trees. Even the lack of food is not a problem. The monarchs do not need to eat. They can live off their stored fat. The cooler temperatures help also. The butterflies use less energy when it is cool.

The butterflies warm up enough to fly on sunny days. They go to a stream for a drink. Or they drop to the ground to sip dew from plants. The butterflies return to the trees as soon as a cloud passes over. Being away from the trees is unsafe. There is danger on the ground. Predators may catch the butterflies. Or the butterflies can get wet and freeze to death.

*Resting in forest trees
during winter
keeps monarchs
safe from cold.*

It takes several generations of monarchs for the butterflies to reach their summer homes.

FLYING BACK NORTH

The days grow longer and warmer as winter passes. Soon the monarchs become active again. They leave the forests in the second week of March. They go back the way they came. It is time to make the journey north.

But these butterflies will not travel far. They have already completed a 1,000 to 3,000 mile (1,600 to 4,800 km) trip. Their wings are torn. They have little fat left in their bodies. They have lived 8 or 9 months. That is a long life for a butterfly. But now their lives are coming to an end. There is one last thing they must do. They must mate. Then the females find milkweed plants to lay their eggs. After that, the adult butterflies die.

But the migration is not over. The return trip is like a relay. Their children will fly next in the migration. The caterpillars hatch and begin to grow. Soon they become adult butterflies. They continue flying north. These butterflies do not live as long as their parents. They live about a month. But as they fly north they mate. And the females lay eggs. Then they die. Their children will continue the trip.

Two or three more groups of monarchs are born. The last group reaches the monarch's summer homes. The butterflies arrive just as the milkweed has started to grow in the north. Millions and millions of monarchs arrive in the summer. They fly in fields, meadows, and gardens again.

In spring, butterflies return to meadows in the north.

HABITAT THREATS

The monarch's migration has changed in the last 100 years. People have caused these changes.

People have destroyed the monarch's summer habitats. They have built roads, houses, and farms in the fields and meadows. Many people think milkweed plants are weeds. They mow milkweed and wildflowers that grow along roads. They spray the plants with a liquid that kills the plants. Without milkweed, monarch caterpillars cannot grow. Without flowers, monarch butterflies cannot eat.

The California forests where monarchs spend the winter have changed. Today monarchs roost in eucalyptus, pine, and cypress trees. Long ago they also roosted in sycamore trees. The sycamores have almost disappeared. They have been cut down. Many worry that the western monarchs' winter home will be destroyed.

There are more problems in the oyamel forests. The eastern monarchs gather in only about 12 places. There can be 100 million monarchs each winter. Any changes can affect the monarchs in a big way. The streams in the forest go dry because people use too much water. Monarchs have to fly farther to find water to drink. Sometimes they cannot make it back to the trees before the cold weather returns.

The oyamel forests are in danger of being destroyed. The oyamel trees are being cut down. This opens gaps in the forest. The gaps let in snow and rain. This can be deadly for the insects.

All of these changes make the Mexican forests unsafe for monarchs. More butterflies are dying than before.

Sycamore and other trees monarchs use for homes are being cut down.

SCIENTISTS FOUND THE
MEXICAN WINTER SITES OF
THE MONARCH IN 1975.
UNTIL THEN, ONLY LOCAL
VILLAGERS KNEW ABOUT THE
BUTTERFLIES' WINTER HOMES.

Butterfly gardens help monarchs find the food they need.

People from Mexico, the United States, and Canada must work together to solve the monarchs' problems. Scientists study the monarchs. They try to learn how many monarchs are alive each year. They try to understand what harms the butterflies. And they try to find answers. Scientists tell the world about the need to save the monarch butterfly.

In Mexico, people must take care of the forests. They must stop others from cutting down the oyamel trees. In the United States and Canada, people must work to save monarch's habitats.

Many people have already planted butterfly gardens. These gardens are filled with milkweed and nectar plants. They provide food for caterpillars and adult butterflies. They have flowers that bloom during the spring and fall migrations. These gardens act like stepping stones across a stream for the monarchs. They give monarchs places to stop, eat, and continue their journey. These patches of habitat help monarchs survive and continue their glorious migration.

TYPES OF MIGRATION

Different animals migrate for different reasons. Some move because of the climate. Some travel to find food or a mate. Here are the different types of animal migration:

Seasonal migration: This type of migration happens when the seasons change. Most animals migrate for this reason. Other types of migration, such as altitudinal and latitudinal, may also include seasonal migration.

Latitudinal migration: When animals travel north and south, it is called latitudinal migration. Doing so allows animals to change the climate where they live.

Altitudinal migration: This migration happens when animals move up and down mountains. In summer, animals can live higher on a mountain. During the cold winter, they move down to lower and warmer spots.

Reproductive migration: Sometimes animals move to have their babies. This migration may keep the babies safer when they are born. Or babies may need a certain habitat to live in after birth.

Nomadic migration: Animals may wander from place to place to find food in this type of migration.

Complete migration: This type of migration happens when animals are finished mating in an area. Then almost all of the animals leave the area. They may travel more than 15,000 miles (25,000 km) to spend winters in a warmer area.

Partial migration: When some, but not all, animals of one type move away from their mating area, it is partial migration. This is the most common type of migration.

Irruptive migration: This type of migration may happen one year, but not the next. It may include some or all of a type of animal. And the animal group may travel short or long distances.

> SOMETIMES ANIMALS NEVER COME BACK TO A PLACE WHERE THEY ONCE LIVED. THIS CAN HAPPEN WHEN HUMANS OR NATURE DESTROY THEIR HABITAT. FOOD, WATER, OR SHELTER MAY BECOME HARD TO FIND. OR A GROUP OF ANIMALS MAY BECOME TOO LARGE FOR AN AREA. THEN THEY MUST MOVE TO FIND FOOD.

GLOSSARY

antennae (an-TEN-ee): Antennae are thin feelers on an insect's head. A monarch butterfly has antennae.

basks (BASKS): A butterfly basks when it spreads its wings to take in heat from the sunshine. A monarch butterfly basks in the sun.

chrysalis (KRISS-uh-liss): A chrysalis is a butterfly in the stage between caterpillar and adult. Inside a chrysalis is a pupa.

habitat (HAB-uh-tat): A habitat is a place that has the food, water, and shelter an animal needs to survive. The monarch's summer habitat has milkweed plants.

hatches (HACH-ez): An animal hatches when it breaks out of its egg. A monarch caterpillar hatches on a milkweed plant.

host plant (HOHST PLANT): A host plant is a plant that is used for food for new caterpillars. The monarch's host plant is the milkweed plant.

metamorphosis (met-uh-MOR-fuh-siss): Metamorphosis is the series of changes some animals go through between hatching and adulthood. A monarch butterfly goes through a metamorphosis from larva to adult.

molts (MOLTS): When a caterpillar molts, it sheds old skin and grows new skin. A monarch caterpillar molts a few times.

nectar (NEK-tur): Nectar is a sweet liquid produced by flowers. Monarch butterflies drink nectar for food.

population (pop-yuh-LAY-shuhn): A population is all the animals of one type that live in the same area. A monarch butterfly population flies to the oyamel forests.

predators (PRED-uh-turs): Predators are animals that hunt and eat other animals. Colors on a monarch's body tell predators to stay away.

proboscis (pro-BOHS-is): A proboscis is the tongue of a butterfly that curls up. A butterfly drinks nectar with its proboscis.

pupa (PYOO-puh): A pupa is an insect in the life cycle stage between larva and adult. A monarch pupa changes in its chrysalis.

seasonal (SEE-zuhn-uhl): Seasonal is something related to the seasons of the year. Monarch butterflies have a seasonal migration.

FURTHER INFORMATION

Books

Burris, Judy, and Wayne Richards. *The Life Cycles of Butterflies: From Egg to Maturity, a Visual Guide to 23 Common Garden Butterflies.* North Adams, MA: Storey Publishing, 2006.

Kalman, Bobbie. *The Life Cycle of a Butterfly.* New York: Crabtree Publishing. 2005.

Stewart, Melissa. *A Place for Butterflies.* Atlanta: Peachtree Publishers. 2006.

Web Sites

Visit our Web site for links about monarch butterfly migration: *childsworld.com/links*

Note to Parents, Teachers, and Librarians:

We routinely verify our Web links to make sure they are safe and active sites. So encourage your readers to check them out!

INDEX

bodies, 9–11, 13, 15, 17, 23

butterfly gardens, 9, 24, 29

caterpillar, 8, 9, 11, 24, 25, 29

chrysalis, 11

eating, 9, 11, 13, 15, 18, 20, 25, 29

eggs, 8, 9, 12, 13, 15, 23, 24

flying, 4, 6, 13, 15, 17, 20, 23–24, 26

mating, 13, 15, 23, 24

metamorphosis, 9

migration route, 6, 17

milkweed, 8, 9, 11, 12, 13, 23, 24, 25, 29

oyamel trees, 18, 20, 26, 29

predators, 11, 20

pupa, 11

roosting, 16, 25

senses, 13, 17

summer homes, 13, 15, 24, 25

threats, 25–29

winter homes, 6, 13, 17, 18–20, 23, 25, 26, 27